How to spread the Gospel

Advice and encouragement
from Pope Benedict XVI

Compiled by
Fr Donncha Ó hAodha

*All booklets are published thanks to the
generous support of the members of the
Catholic Truth Society*

CATHOLIC TRUTH SOCIETY
PUBLISHERS TO THE HOLY SEE

Contents

A virtual dialogue

During and since the Second Vatican Council, the Church has vigorously reaffirmed her essentially missionary nature and the consequent apostolic responsibility of each and every baptized person[1]. Perhaps for many of the faithful, this aspect of their baptismal vocation still needs to be put into practice. In the exercise of his ministry, Benedict XVI frequently proposes the fundamental right and duty of all Christians to be apostles. During his visit to the United Kingdom in September 2010, the Holy Father repeatedly encouraged Catholics, especially the lay faithful, to live out their prophetic calling in daily life and in the public square. His teaching on this topic is characteristically rich, accessible and encouraging.

What follows is an imaginary dialogue. The questions posed are those which any Catholic might ask on considering his or her call to spread the faith. The responses offered are taken from different instances of the preaching of the Holy Father.

Why should I evangelize?

On one occasion when Christ looked upon the people who had come to listen to him, seeking some guidance from him, he felt compassion for them, because they were like sheep without a shepherd (cf. *Mk* 6:34). Amid the contradictory messages of that time, they did not know which way to turn. What great compassion he must feel in our own time too – on account of all the endless talk that people hide behind, while in reality they are totally confused. Where must we go? What are the values by which we can order our lives? The values by which we can educate our young, without giving them norms they may be unable to resist, or demanding of them things that perhaps should not be imposed upon them? He is the Light.[2]

Faith is meant to bear fruit in the transformation of our world through the power of the Holy Spirit at work in the lives and activities of believers. No one who looks realistically at our world today could think that Christians can afford to go on with business as usual, ignoring the profound crisis of faith which has overtaken our society, or simply trusting that the patrimony of values handed down by Christian centuries will continue to inspire and shape the future of our society. We know that in times of crisis and upheaval God has raised up great saints and prophets for the renewal of the Church and Christian society; we trust in his providence and we pray for his continual guidance. But each of us, in accordance with his or her state of life, is called to work for the advancement of God's Kingdom by imbuing temporal life with the values of the Gospel. Each of us has a mission, each of us is called to change the world, to work for a culture of life, a culture forged by love and respect for the dignity of each human person. As our Lord tells us ... our light must shine in the sight of all, so that seeing our good works, they may give praise to our heavenly Father (cf. *Mt* 5:16).[3]

Not only youth, but also communities and the Pastors themselves must become more and more aware of a fundamental fact about evangelization: wherever God does not have pride of place, wherever he is not recognized and worshipped as the Supreme Good, human dignity is at risk.[4]

Why am I not always successful in my apostolic efforts?

Indeed, I have come among you above all to encourage you to be daring witnesses of Christ. It is trusting adherence to his Word that will make your pastoral efforts fruitful. When work in the Lord's vineyard seems to have been in vain like the nightlong efforts of the Apostles, you must never forget that Jesus can reverse everything in an instant.[5]

Anyone who has come across something true, beautiful and good in his life - the one true treasure, the precious pearl - hastens to share it everywhere, in the family and at work, in all the contexts of his life.

He does so without any fear, because he knows he has received adoption as a son; without any presumption, for it is all a gift; without discouragement, for God's Spirit precedes his action in people's "hearts" and as a seed in the most diverse cultures and religions.

He does so without restraint, for he bears a piece of good news which is for all people and for all the peoples.

Dear friends, I ask you to collaborate even more, very much more, in the Pope's universal apostolic ministry, opening doors to Christ ...

The Holy Spirit gives believers a superior vision of the world, of life, of history, and makes them custodians of the hope that never disappoints.[6]

How can one persevere in the face of difficulties?

The task of proclamation and the call to suffer for Christ's sake are inseparable ... In a world in which falsehood is powerful; the truth is paid for with suffering. The one who desires to avoid suffering, to keep it at bay, keeps life itself and its greatness at bay; he cannot be a servant of truth and thus a servant of faith. There is no love without suffering - without the suffering of renouncing oneself, of the transformation and purification of self for true freedom. Where there is nothing worth suffering for, even life loses its value.[7]

Today, as yesterday, Christian life demands the courage to go against the tide, to love like Jesus, who even went so far as to sacrifice himself on the Cross.[8]

There is no doubt that following Christ is difficult, but, as he says, only those who lose their life for his sake and the Gospel's will save it (cf. *Mk* 8:35), giving full meaning to their existence.[9]

Our great hope as believers is eternal life in communion with Christ and the whole family of God. This great hope gives us the strength to face and to overcome the difficulties of life in this world.[10]

Is spreading the knowledge of Christ worthwhile?

We must return to proclaiming powerfully and joyfully the event of Christ's death and Resurrection, heart of Christianity, principal fulcrum of our faith, powerful lever of our certainty, impetuous wind that sweeps away every fear and indecision, every doubt and human calculation.[11]

The task of the shepherd, the task of the fisher of men, can often seem wearisome. But it is beautiful and wonderful, because it is truly a service to joy, to God's joy which longs to break into the world.[12]

Christ is always with us and always walks with his Church, accompanies her and guards her, as he has told us: "I am with you always, to the close of the age" (*Mt*

28:20). Never doubt his presence! Always seek the Lord Jesus, grow in friendship with him, and receive him in communion. Learn to listen to his word and also to recognize him in the poor. Live your lives with joy and enthusiasm, sure of his presence and of his unconditional, generous friendship, faithful even to death on the cross. Bear witness to all of the joy that his strong yet gentle presence evokes, starting with your contemporaries. Tell them that it is beautiful to be a friend of Jesus and that it is well worth following him. With your enthusiasm, demonstrate that, among all the different ways of life that the world today seems to offer us – apparently all on the same level – the only way in which we find the true meaning of life and hence true and lasting joy, is by following Jesus.[13]

Why is evangelization a "service to joy"?

Joy is the expression of being in harmony with oneself, and this can derive only from being in harmony with God and with his creation.[14]

Born in the poverty of the manger, Jesus comes to offer to all that joy and that peace which alone can fulfill the expectations of the human soul.[15]

The mystery of Bethlehem reveals to us God-with-us, the God close to us and not merely in the spatial and temporal sense; he is close to us because he has, as it were, "espoused" our humanity; he has taken our condition upon himself, choosing to be like us in all things save sin in order to make us become like him. Christian joy thus springs from this certainty: God is close, he is with me, and he is with us, in joy and in sorrow, in sickness and in health, as a friend and faithful spouse. And this joy endures, even in trials, in suffering itself. It does not remain only on the surface; it dwells in the depths of the person who entrusts himself to God and trusts in him.

Some people ask: but is this joy still possible today? Men and women of every age and social condition, happy to dedicate their existence to others, give us the answer with their lives![16]

Are there words of encouragement?

The Church's evangelizing mission is the response to the cry "Come, Lord Jesus" that pervades all of salvation history and continues to rise from believers' lips. Come, Lord, transform our hearts, so that justice and peace may be spread in the world …

Nothing is more beautiful, urgent and important than freely offering to men and women, in turn, what we ourselves have freely received from God! Nothing can dispense or relieve us from this burdensome but fascinating commitment …

The Virgin Mary, who did not communicate to the world an idea but Jesus, the Incarnate Word, is an unparalleled model of evangelization. Let us invoke her with trust so that, in our time too, the Church may proclaim Christ, the Saviour. May every Christian and every community feel the joy of sharing with others the Good News that "God so loved the world that he gave his Only Son ... that the world might be saved through him" (*Jn* 3:16-17).[17]

Dear brothers and sisters ... lift up your eyes to ... Our Lady ... The angel of the Annunciation greeted Mary as "full of grace", signifying with this expression that her heart and her life were totally open to God and, as such, completely permeated by his grace. May Our Lady help you to make yourselves a free and total "Yes" to the grace of God, so that you can be renewed and thus renew humanity by the light and the joy of the Holy Spirit.[18]

Seek daily the protection of Mary, Mother of the Lord and mirror of all holiness. She, the all-holy one, will help you to be faithful disciples of her Son Jesus Christ.[19]

Who is called to evangelize?

You need to become witnesses with me to the resurrection of Jesus. In effect, if you do not become his witnesses in your daily lives, who will do so in your place? Christians are, in the Church and with the Church, missionaries of Christ sent into the world.[20]

Am I called to spread the Faith?

Every Christian is called through Baptism and Confirmation to proclaim Christ, the light of the world, in word and in the witness of his life.[21]

How important it is that we Christians are faithful to our vocation! Every authentic believer is always travelling his own personal itinerary of faith, and at the same time, with the little light that he carries within himself, can and must be a help to those alongside him, and even help the one for whom finding the way that leads to Christ is difficult.[22]

For Christians ... the words of St Paul are valid: "The love of Christ impels us" (2 *Co* 5:14). The charity that moved the Father to send his Son into the world, and moved the Son to offer himself for us even to death on the Cross, that same charity has been poured out by the Holy Spirit in the hearts of believers.

12

Every baptized person, as a vine united to the branch, can therefore cooperate in the mission of Jesus, which can be summarized thus: to bring to every person the good news that "God is love" and … to save the world.

The mission arises from the heart: when one stops to pray before a Crucifix with his glance fixed on that pierced side, he cannot but experience within himself the joy of knowing that he is loved and the desire to love and to make himself an instrument of mercy and reconciliation.[23]

Why am I expected to do more than save my own soul?

Christ's presence is a gift that we must be able to share with everyone.[24]

How could Christians keep for themselves alone what they have received? How could they hoard this treasure and bury this spring? The Church's mission is not to preserve power, or to gain wealth; her mission is to offer Christ, to give a share in Christ's own life, man's most precious good, which God himself gives us in his Son.[25]

Faith demands to be passed on: it was not given to us merely for ourselves, for the personal salvation of our own souls, but for others, for this world and for our time. We must bring faith into this world so that it may become in it a living force; in order to increase God's presence in the world.[26]

We must overcome the temptation to restrict ourselves to what we already have, or think we have, safely in our possession: it would be sure death in terms of the Church's presence in the world; the Church, for that matter, can only be missionary, in the outward movement of the Spirit. From its origins, the Christian people have clearly recognized the importance of communicating the Good News of Jesus to those who did not yet know him.[27]

Is doing apostolate just for people with a special missionary calling?

Anyone who has discovered Christ must lead others to him. A great joy cannot be kept to oneself. It has to be passed on.[28]

The rediscovery of the value of one's own Baptism is at the root of every Christian's missionary commitment, because as we see in the Gospel, those who allow themselves to be fascinated by Christ cannot fail to witness to the joy of following in his footsteps ... It is precisely in virtue of Baptism that we possess a co-natural missionary vocation ... May every baptized person, closely united to the Lord, feel that he is called to proclaim God's love to everyone with the witness of his own life.[29]

I am imperfect so how can I preach to others?

It is the Word, certainly not us, that illumines, purifies and converts. We are merely servants of the Word of life.[30]

To transform the world, God chose a humble young girl from a village in Galilee, Mary of Nazareth, and challenged her with this greeting: "Hail, full of grace, the Lord is with you" ... God repeats these words to the Church, to each one of us: Rejoice, the Lord is close! With Mary's help, let us offer ourselves with humility and courage so that the world may accept Christ, who is the source of true joy.[31]

What is the message I should be spreading?

This Good News is not just a word, but a person, Christ himself, risen and alive! By the grace of the sacraments, the water flowing from his open side on the Cross has become an overflowing spring, "rivers of living water", a flood that no one can halt, a gift that restores life.[32]

In Jesus Christ the road to salvation has been shown to all people, a salvation that is first of all spiritual redemption, but that involves the entire human, including the social and historical, dimensions.[33]

Do I have to explain Christ's teachings to others?

How necessary it is at the beginning of this third millennium that the entire Christian community, unanimously and of one accord, proclaim, teach and witness to the full to the truths of the Catholic faith, doctrine and morals! May the *Compendium* of the *Catechism of the Catholic Church* also contribute to the hoped for renewal of catechesis and evangelization so that all Christians - children, young people, adults, families and communities -, docile to the action of the Holy Spirit, may become catechists and evangelizers in every environment, helping others to encounter Christ. We ask this with trust in the Virgin Mother of God, Star of Evangelization.[34]

What better goal could teachers of religion set themselves than Blessed John Henry Newman's famous appeal for an intelligent, well-instructed laity: "I want a laity, not arrogant, not rash in speech, not disputatious, but men who know their religion, who enter into it, who know just where they stand, who know what they hold and what they do not, who know their creed so well that they can give an account of it, who know so much of history that they can defend it (*The Present Position of Catholics in England*, ix, 390) … I pray that, through his intercession and example, all who are engaged in the task of teaching and catechesis will be inspired to greater effort by the vision he so clearly sets before us.[35]

Do I have to proclaim unpopular teachings about death and the afterlife?

One of the greatest challenges facing us today is how to speak convincingly of the wisdom and liberating power of God's word to a world which all too often sees the Gospel as a constriction of human freedom, instead of the truth which liberates our minds and enlightens our efforts to live wisely and well, both as individuals and members of society.[36]

Jesus turns directly to the Twelve and asks them: "Will you also go away?" (*Jn* 6:67). This provocative question is not only addressed to listeners in his time, but also reaches the believers and people of every epoch. Today too, many are "shocked" by the paradox of the Christian faith. Jesus' teaching seems "hard", too difficult to accept and to put into practice. Then there are those who reject it and abandon Christ; there are those who seek to "adapt" his word to the fashions of the times, misrepresenting its meaning and value. "Will you also go away?" This disturbing provocation resounds in our hearts and expects a personal answer from each one; it is a question addressed to each one of us. Jesus is not content with superficial and formal belonging, a first and enthusiastic adherence is not enough for him; on the contrary, what is necessary is to take part for one's whole life "in his thinking and in his willing". Following him fills our hearts with joy and gives full meaning to our existence, but it entails difficulties and sacrifices because very often we must swim against the tide.[37]

The Apostle Paul, writing to the first communities, exhorted the faithful to "not grieve as others do who have no hope. For since", he wrote, "we believe that Jesus died and rose again, even so, through Jesus, God will bring with him those who have fallen asleep" (1 *Th* 4:13-14). Today too, it is necessary to evangelize about the reality of death and eternal life, realities particularly subject to superstitious beliefs and syncretisms, so that the Christian truth does not risk mixing itself with myths of various types.[38]

Why are the moral elements of the Gospel so unpopular?

God's Commandments are not obstacles to freedom and to a beautiful life, but signposts on the road on which to travel to find life.[39]

The Law, like a word of love, is not a contradiction of freedom but a renewal from within by means of friendship with God.[40]

The announcement of the Ten Commandments is introduced by a significant reference to the liberation of the People of Israel. The text says: "I am the Lord your God, who brought you out of the land of Egypt, out of the house of bondage" (*Ex* 20:2).

Thus, the Decalogue is intended as a confirmation of the freedom gained. Indeed, at a closer look, the Commandments are the means that the Lord gives us to protect our freedom, both from the internal conditioning of passions and from the external abuse of those with evil intentions. The "no's" of the Commandments are as many "yeses" to the growth of true freedom.[41]

The Ten Commandments are first and foremost a "yes" to God, to a God who loves us and leads us, who carries us and yet allows us our freedom: indeed, it is he who makes our freedom real (the first three commandments). It is a "yes" to the family (fourth commandment), a "yes" to life (fifth commandment), a "yes" to responsible love (sixth commandment), a "yes" to solidarity, to social responsibility and to justice (seventh commandment), a "yes" to truth (eighth commandment) and a "yes" to respect for other people and for what is theirs (ninth and tenth commandments). By the strength of our friendship with the living God we live this manifold "yes" and at the same time we carry it as a signpost into this world of ours today.[42]

The word of God is a word of unbounded hope. "God loved the world so much that he gave his only Son … so that through him, the world might be saved" (*Jn* 3:16-17). God does not give up on us! He continues to lift our eyes to a future of hope, and he promises us the strength to accomplish it. As Saint Paul tells us … God created us in Christ Jesus "to live the good life", a life of good deeds, in accordance with his will (cf. *Ep* 2:10). He gave us his commandments, not as a burden, but as a source of freedom: the freedom to become men and women of wisdom, teachers of justice and peace, people who believe in others and seek their authentic good. God created us to live in the light, and to be light for the world around us![43]

Why are some people so closed to God?

When contemporary man proclaims his total autonomy from God, he enslaves himself and often finds himself in comfortless loneliness.[44]

Human beings cannot completely fulfill themselves, they cannot be truly happy without God.[45]

Without God, man loses his grandeur; without God, there is no true humanism.[46]

Only where God is seen does life truly begin. Only when we meet the living God in Christ do we know what life is. We are not some casual and meaningless product of evolution. Each of us is the result of a thought of God. Each of us is willed, each of us is loved, each of us is necessary. There is nothing more beautiful than to be surprised by the Gospel, by the encounter with Christ. There is nothing more beautiful than to know Him and to speak to others of our friendship with Him.[47]

Even today, as in St Augustine's time, humanity needs to know and above all to live this fundamental reality: God is love, and the encounter with him is the only response to the restlessness of the human heart; a heart inhabited by hope, still perhaps obscure and unconscious in many of our contemporaries but which already today opens us Christians to the future, so much so that St Paul wrote that "in this hope we were saved" (*Rm* 8: 24).[48]

The question is: is the humanity of our time still waiting for a Saviour? One has the feeling that many consider God as foreign to their own interests. Apparently, they do not need him. They live as though he did not exist and, worse still, as though he were an "obstacle" to remove in order to fulfil themselves. Even among believers - we are sure of it - some let themselves be attracted by enticing dreams and distracted by misleading doctrines that suggest deceptive shortcuts to happiness.

Yet, despite its contradictions, worries and tragedies, and perhaps precisely because of them, humanity today seeks a path of renewal, of salvation, it seeks a Saviour and awaits, sometimes unconsciously, the coming of the Saviour who renews the world and our life, the coming of Christ, the one true Redeemer of man and of the whole of man.[49]

Previously, it was thought and believed that by setting God aside and being autonomous, following only our own ideas and inclinations, we would truly be free to do whatever we liked without anyone being able to give us orders. But when God disappears, men and women do not become greater; indeed, they lose the divine dignity, their faces lose God's splendour. In the end, they turn out to be merely products of a blind evolution and, as such, can be used and abused. This is precisely what the experience of our epoch has confirmed for us.

Only if God is great is humankind also great. With Mary, we must begin to understand that this is so. We must not drift away from God but make God present; we must ensure that he is great in our lives. Thus, we too will become divine; all the splendour of the divine dignity will then be ours. Let us apply this to our own lives.

... Let us make God great in public and in private life. This means making room for God in our lives every day, starting in the morning with prayers, and then dedicating time to God, giving Sundays to God. We do not waste our free time if we offer it to God. If God enters into our time, all time becomes greater, roomier, and richer.[50]

Why don't I just let other people believe what they want?

Believing is not adding one opinion to others. And the conviction, the belief, that God exists is not information like any other. Regarding most information, it makes no difference to us whether it is true or false; it does not change our lives. But if God does not exist, life is empty, the future is empty. And if God exists, everything changes, life is light, our future is light and we have guidance for how to live. Therefore, believing constitutes the fundamental orientation of our life. To believe, to say: "Yes, I believe that you are God, I believe that you are present among us in the Incarnate Son", gives my life a direction, impels me to be attached to God, to unite with God and so to find my dwelling place, and the way to live.[51]

Man is not fulfilled in an absolute autonomy, deceiving himself that he is God but, on the contrary, by recognizing himself as a child, an open creature, reaching out to God and to his brethren in whose faces he discovers the image of their common Father.[52]

Those who cast God aside do not make man great but divest him of his dignity. Man then becomes a failed product of evolution. Those who accuse God also accuse man. Faith in God defends man in all his frailty and short-comings: God's brightness shines on every individual.[53]

In fact, it is not God's presence that alienates man but his absence: without the true God, Father of the Lord Jesus Christ, illusory hopes become an invitation to escape from reality. Speaking with God, dwelling in his presence, letting oneself be illuminated and purified by his Word introduces us, instead, into the heart of reality, into the very motor of becoming cosmic; it introduces us, so to speak, to the beating heart of the universe.[54]

Yes, my dear brothers and sisters, converting to love means passing from bitterness to "sweetness", from sorrow to true joy. Man is truly himself and fulfils himself completely to the extent that he lives with God and of God, recognizing him and loving him in his brethren.[55]

Here we are speaking of spiritual realities - why can't we just help people materially?

Social issues and the Gospel are inseparable. When we bring people only knowledge, ability, technical competence and tools, we bring them too little.[56]

God alone is the redemption of man. And we can see in the history of the last century that in those nations where God was abolished, not only was the economy destroyed, but above all the souls.

Moral destruction and the destruction of human dignity are fundamental forms of destruction, and renewal can only come from God's return, that is, from recognition of God's centrality.

A Bishop from the Congo on an *ad limina* visit in these days said to me: Europeans generously give us many things for development, but there is a hesitation in helping us in pastoral ministry; it seems as though they considered pastoral ministry useless, that only technological and material development were important. But the contrary is true, he said; where the Word of God does not exist, development fails to function and has no positive results. Only if God's Word is put first, only if man is reconciled with God, can material things also go smoothly.[57]

Faith is born from the personal encounter with the Risen Christ and becomes an impulse of courage and freedom that makes one cry to the world: "Jesus is risen and alive for ever".

This is the mission of the Lord's disciples in every epoch and also in our time: "If, then, you have been raised with Christ", St Paul exhorts us, "seek the things that are above ... Set your minds on things that are above, not on things that are on earth" (*Col* 3:1-2). This does not mean cutting oneself off from one's daily commitments, neglecting earthly realities; rather, it means reviving every human activity with a supernatural breath, it means making ourselves joyful proclaimers and witnesses of the Resurrection of Christ, living for eternity (cf. *Jn* 20:25; *Lk* 24:33-34).[58]

We must make the tenderness of God's Heart felt, especially by the weakest and neediest people; and do not forget that in spreading divine love, each one of us makes a contribution to building a more just and supportive world.[59]

How should a Christian spread the Gospel?

Is it simply a matter of getting the right structures in place?

Some think at times that missionary effectiveness depends primarily on careful programming and its subsequent intelligent application through a concrete commitment.

The Lord certainly does ask for our collaboration, but before any other response his initiative is necessary: his Spirit is the true protagonist of the Church. The roots of our being and of our action are in the wise and provident silence of God.[60]

The exhausting yet sterile nocturnal fishing of the disciples is a perennial warning for the Church of all ages: alone, without Jesus, we can do nothing! In apostolic tasks our own forces do not suffice; even if our work is well organized it proves ineffective without divine Grace.[61]

Yes! We are called to serve the humanity of our own time, trusting in Jesus alone, letting ourselves be enlightened by his word: "You did not choose me, but I chose you and appointed you that you should go and bear fruit and that your fruit should abide" (*Jn* 15:16).

How much time we have lost, how must work has been set back, on account of our lack of attention to this point! Everything is to be defined starting with Christ, as far as the origins and effectiveness of mission is concerned: we receive mission always from Christ, who has made known to us what he has heard from his Father, and we are appointed to mission through the Spirit, in the Church. Like the Church herself, which is the work of Christ and his Spirit, it is a question of renewing the face of the earth starting from God, God always and alone.[62]

How can we help others become friends with Jesus?

In order to become fishers of men with Christ one first needs to be "caught" by him.[63]

Help people to discover the true star which points out the way to us: Jesus Christ! Let us seek to know him better and better, so as to be able to guide others to him with conviction.[64]

Entering into the sentiments of Jesus: this should be our daily practice of living as Christians.[65]

What counts is to place Jesus Christ at the centre of our lives, so that our identity is marked essentially by the encounter, by communion with Christ and with his Word. In his light every other value is recovered and purified from possible dross.[66]

How do I achieve this in practice?

To be a disciple and a missionary implies a close bond with the Word of God, the Eucharist and the other sacraments, in order to live in the Church in obedient listening to her teachings.

To renew with joy the will to be Jesus' disciples, to "remain with him", this is the fundamental condition to being a missionary.[67]

The Eucharist, in effect, is the driving force of the Church's entire evangelizing action, a little like the heart in the human body.[68]

How very significant is the bond between the Church's mission and the Eucharist. In fact, missionary and evangelizing action is the apostolic diffusion of love that is, as it were, concentrated in the Most Blessed Sacrament.[69]

Is prayer important in this context?

Actually, praying for others is a great act of charity.[70]

The first missionary commitment of each one of us is prayer. It is first and foremost in praying that the way is prepared for the Gospel; it is in praying that hearts are opened to the mystery of God and souls disposed to welcome his Word of Salvation.[71]

In private as well as in community, we must pray very much for vocations, so that the greatness and the beauty of the love of God may attract many to follow Christ on the path of priesthood and in consecrated life. Equally, we must also pray so that there may be saintly spouses, able to show their children, especially through their example, the lofty horizons to strive for with their freedom. The saints, men and women, that the Church proposes for veneration by all the faithful, testify to the ripened fruit of this interweaving between the Divine calling and the human response. Let us entrust our prayer for vocations to their heavenly intercession.[72]

Do we have to live faith in action?

As Pope Paul VI rightly noted, "modern man listens more willingly to witnesses than to teachers, and if he does listen to teachers, it is because they are witnesses".[73]

How much contemporary society needs this witness! How much we need, in the Church and in society, witnesses of the beauty of holiness, witnesses of the splendour of truth, witnesses of the joy and freedom born of a living relationship with Christ![74]

This is important: faith is not only thought but also touches the whole of our being. Since God became Man in flesh and blood, since he entered the tangible world, we must seek and encounter God in all the dimensions of our being. Thus the reality of God, through faith, penetrates our being and transforms it.[75]

Jesus did not come to teach us philosophy but to show us a way, indeed *the* way that leads to life. This way is love which is an expression of true faith. If someone loves his neighbour with a pure and generous heart it means that he truly knows God. If instead someone says he has faith but does not love his brethren, he is not a true believer. God does not dwell within him.[76]

If we have accepted the truth of Christ and committed our lives to him, there can be no separation between what we believe and the way we live our lives. Our every thought, word and action must be dedicated to the glory of God and the spread of his Kingdom ... Truth is passed on not merely by formal teaching, important as that is, but also by the witness of lives lived in integrity, fidelity and holiness; those who live in and by the truth instinctively recognize what is false and, precisely as false, inimical to the beauty and goodness which accompany the splendour of truth, *veritatis splendor*.[77]

To be a witness of Jesus Christ means above all to bear witness to a certain way of living. ... "We know and believe the love God has for us" (1 *Jn* 4:16). Yes, man can believe in love. Let us bear witness to our faith in such a way that it shines forth as the power of love, "so that the world may believe" (*Jn* 17:21).[78]

Praying fervently for the coming of the Kingdom also means being constantly alert for the signs of its presence, and working for its growth in every sector of society. It means facing the challenges of present and future with confidence in Christ's victory and a commitment to extending his reign. It means not losing heart in the face of resistance, adversity and scandal. It means overcoming every separation between faith and life, and countering false gospels of freedom and happiness. It also means rejecting a false dichotomy between faith and political life, since, as the Second Vatican Council put it, "there is no human activity – even in secular affairs – which can be withdrawn from God's dominion" (*Lumen Gentium*, 36).[79]

Let us allow the paschal "alleluia" to be deeply impressed within us too, so that it is not only a word in certain external circumstances but is expressed in our own lives, the lives of people who invite everyone to praise the Lord and do so with their behaviour as "risen" ones. "Pray the Lord for us", we say to Mary, that the One who restored joy to the whole world by means of his Son's Resurrection may grant us to enjoy such gladness now and always, in our life and in the life without end.[80]

What behavior would attract others to Christ?

This is what disciples of Christ must do: trained by him to live in the way of the Beatitudes, they must attract all people to God through a witness of love: "In the same way, your light must shine before men so that they may see goodness in your deeds and give praise to your heavenly Father" (*Mt* 5:16).[81]

To live Christian love, means at the same time to introduce God's light into the world and to point out its true source. Saint Leo the Great writes: "Whoever, in fact, lives a holy and chaste life in the Church, whoever sets his mind on things that are above, not on things that are on earth (cf. *Col* 3:2), in a certain way resembles heavenly light; as long as he himself observes the brilliance of a holy life, he shows to many, like a star, the path that leads to God" (*Sermon* III:5).[82]

Loving, Jesus says, means acting like the Good Samaritan. And we know that he himself is the Good Samaritan par excellence; although he was God, he did not hesitate to humble himself to the point of becoming a man and giving his life for us.

Love is therefore the "heart" of Christian life; indeed, love alone, awakened in us by the Holy Spirit, makes us Christ's witnesses.[83]

"We know and believe the love God has for us". We have believed in love: this is the essence of Christianity … Love is the essence of Christianity, which makes the believer and the Christian community a leaven of hope and peace in every environment and especially attentive to the needs of the poor and needy. This is our common mission: to be a leaven of hope and peace because we believe in love. Love makes the Church live, and since it is eternal it makes her live for ever, to the end of time.[84]

Where should I try to spread the Gospel?

Christ continues to send his disciples into the world in order to proclaim the coming of his Kingdom and to bring his peace into the world, beginning house by house, family by family, town by town.[85]

In our daily lives, dear friends, there are so many opportunities to proclaim this faith of ours to others simply and with conviction, so that from our encounter their faith can grow.

And it is more urgent than ever that the men and women of our age know and encounter Jesus, and, also thanks to our example, allow themselves to be won over by him.[86]

Jesus' mission concerns all humanity. Therefore, the Church is given responsibility for all humanity, so that it may recognize God, the God who for all of us was made man in Jesus Christ, suffered, died and was raised.

The Church must never be satisfied with the ranks of those she has reached at a certain point or say that others are fine as they are: Muslims, Hindus and so forth. The Church can never retreat comfortably to within the limits of her own environment. She is charged with universal solicitude; she must be concerned with and for one and all.[87]

Not only non-Christian peoples and those who are far distant await us, but so do social and cultural milieux, and above all human hearts, which are the real goal of the missionary activity of the People of God.[88]

Is promoting the Catholic faith compatible with respect for others beliefs?

We impose nothing, yet we propose ceaselessly, as Peter recommends in one of his Letters: "In your hearts, reverence Christ as Lord. Always be prepared to make a defence to any one who calls you to account for the hope that is in you" (1 *P* 3:15). And everyone, in the end, asks this of us, even those who seem not to. From personal and communal experience, we know well that it is Jesus whom everyone awaits.[89]

We impose our faith on no one. Such proselytism is contrary to Christianity. Faith can develop only in freedom. But we do appeal to the freedom of men and women to open their hearts to God, to seek him, to hear his voice. ... Let us here ask the Lord with all our hearts to speak anew his "*Ephphatha*", to heal our hardness of hearing for God's presence, activity and word, and to give us sight and hearing ...

We do not fail to show respect for other religions and cultures, we do not fail to show profound respect for their faith, when we proclaim clearly and uncompromisingly the God who has countered violence with his own suffering; who in the face of the power of evil exalts his mercy, in order that evil may be limited and overcome.[90]

Today it is up to you ... to offer the Risen Christ to your fellow citizens. So many of them are living in fear of spirits, of malign and threatening powers. In their bewilderment they end up even condemning street children and the elderly as alleged sorcerers. Who can go to them to proclaim that Christ has triumphed over death and all those occult powers (cf. *Ep* 1:19-23; 6:10-12)? Someone may object: "Why not leave them in peace? They have their truth, and we have ours. Let us all try to live in peace, leaving everyone as they are, so they can best be themselves." But if we are convinced and have come to experience that without Christ life lacks something, that something real – indeed, the most real thing of all – is missing, we must also be convinced that we do no injustice to anyone if we present Christ to them and thus grant them the opportunity of finding their truest and most authentic selves, the joy of finding life. Indeed, we must do this. It is our duty to offer everyone this possibility of attaining eternal life.[91]

We too, like Mary Magdalene, Thomas and the other Apostles, are called to be witnesses of Christ's death and Resurrection. We cannot keep this important news to ourselves. We must convey it to the whole world: "We have seen the Lord!" (*Jn* 20:25).[92]

A thank you

Thank you Holy Father for your example and teaching and especially for your faith and joy. We commit ourselves to praying for you in your ministry as Successor of Peter and universal Fisherman. We realize that the dialogue between Peter and the other apostles after Christ's Resurrection, resounds constantly in the Church. In fact it is, in a way, the story of the life of the Church in the world:

'Simon Peter said to them, "I am going fishing." They said to him, "We will go with you."' (*Jn* 21:3)

Endnotes

[1] Cf. Second Vatican Council, *Lumen Gentium*, *Ad Gentes*, and *Apostolicam Actuositatem*. Paul VI, Apostolic Exhortation *Evangelii Nuntiandi*, 8 December 1975; John Paul II, Encyclical *Redemptoris Missio*, 7 December 1990, and Apostolic Exhortation *Christifideles Laici*, 30 December 1988; and Congregation for the Doctrine of the Faith, *Doctrinal Note on some Aspects of Evangelization*, 3 December 2007.

[2] Homily, 11 April 2009.

[3] Homily [Hyde Park, London], 18 September 2010.

[4] Angelus, 28 August 2005.

[5] Homily [Vigevano, Italy], 21 April 2007.

[6] Homily, 3 June 2006.

[7] Homily, 28 June 2008.

[8] Homily [Velletri, Italy], 23 September 2007.

[9] Angelus, 24 September 2006.

[10] Homily, 31 December 2008.

[11] Homily [Verona], 19 October 2006.

[12] Homily [Inauguration of the Pontificate], 24 April 2005.

[13] Homily [Lisbon], 11 May 2010.

[14] Angelus, 25 January 2009.

[15] Audience, 20 December 2006.

[16] Angelus, 16 December 2007.

[17] Angelus, 23 December 2007.

[18] Homily [Oporto, Portugal], 14 May 2010.

[19] Homily [Lisbon], 11 May 2010.

[20] Homily [Oporto, Portugal], 14 May 2010.

[21] Homily, 6 January, 2009.

[22] Angelus, 6 January 2008.

[23] Angelus, 22 October 2006.

38

[24] Homily, 31 December 2008.

[25] Homily [Istanbul], 1 December 2006.

[26] Homily, 12 September 2009.

[27] Homily [Oporto, Portugal], 14 May 2010.

[28] Homily [World Youth Day, Cologne], 21 August 2005.

[29] Angelus, 29 October 2006.

[30] Homily, 6 January 2009.

[31] Angelus, 17 December 2009,

[32] Homily [Istanbul], 1 December 2006.

[33] Angelus, 1 January 2009.

[34] Angelus, 3 July 2005.

[35] Homily [Birmingham], 19 September 2010.

[36] Homily [Westminster Cathedral], 18 September 2010.

[37] Angelus, 23 August 2009.

[38] Angelus, 2 November 2008.

[39] Homily [Rome's juvenial prison], 18 March 2007.

[40] Homily, 30 August 2009.

[41] Homily, 19 March 2006.

[42] Homily [Mariazelle, Austria], 8 September 2007.

[43] Homily [Luanda, Angola], 22 March 2009.

[44] Audience, 6 February 2008.

[45] Homily [Monte Casino], 24 May 2009.

[46] Audience, 8 August 2007.

[47] Homily [Inauguration of the Pontificate], 24 April 2005.

[48] Audience, 27 February 2008.

[49] Audience, 20 December 2006.

[50] Homily, 15 August 2005.

[51] Homily, 15 August 2006.

[52] Homily [Genoa] 18 May 2008.

[53] Homily, 29 September 2007.

[54] Homily, 6 February 2008.

[55] Homily [Assisi], 17 June 2007.

[56] Homily [Munich], 10 September 2006.

[57] Homily, 5 February 2006.

[58] Audience, 19 April 2006.

[59] Angelus, 15 February 2006.

[60] Homily, 4 June 2006.

[61] Homily [Vigevano, Italy], 21 April 2007.

[62] Homily [Oporto, Portugal], 14 May 2010.

[63] Homily [Santa Maria di Leuca, Italy], 14 June 2008.

[64] Homily [World Youth Day, Cologne], 21 August 2005.

[65] Audience, 1 June 2005.

[66] Audience, 25 October 2006.

[67] Audience, 23 May 2007.

[68] Angelus, 2 October 2005.

[69] Angelus, 23 October 2005.

[70] Homily [Velletri, Italy], 23 September 2007.

[71] Angelus [Pompeii], 19 October 2008.

[72] Regina Caeli, 3 May 2009.

[73] *Letter proclaiming a Year for Priests*, 16 June 2009, quoting Paul VI, *Evangelii Nuntiandi* 41.

[74] Homily [Westminster Cathedral], 18 September 2010.

[75] Audience, 3 June 2009.

[76] Angelus, 13 September 2009.

[77] Homily [Hyde Park, London], 18 September 2010.

[78] Homily [Regensburg, Germany], 12 September 2006.

40

[79] Homily [New York], 20 April 2008.

[80] Regina Caeli, 24 March 2008.

[81] Homily, 6 January 2006.

[82] Homily [Lourdes], 13 September 2008.

[83] Angelus, 15 July 2007.

[84] Homily [Velletri, Italy], 23 September 2007.

[85] Homily [Glasgow, Scotland], 16 September 2010.

[86] Regina Caeli, 9 April 2009.

[87] Homily, 7 May 2006.

[88] Homily [Oporto, Portugal], 14 May 2010.

[89] Homily [Oporto, Portugal], 14 May 2010.

[90] Homily [Munich], 10 September 2006.

[91] Homily [Luanda, Angola], 21 March 2009.

[92] Audience, 11 April 2007.